WH
E
INS

BY

VINCENT M. HOLT

WITH AN INTRODUCTION BY

LAURENCE MOUND

Keeper of Entomology
British Museum (Natural History)

'Them insecs eats up every blessed green thing
that do grow, and us farmers starves.'
'Well, eat *them*, and grow fat!'

BRITISH MUSEUM (NATURAL HISTORY)
E. W. CLASSEY LTD

Originally printed 1885.

Reprinted 1967, 1969, 1973, and 1978
by E. W. Classey Ltd, Faringdon, Oxon.

Reprinted with a new Introduction 1988
by British Museum (Natural History),
Cromwell Road, London SW7 5BD

Introduction © British Museum (Natural History)
1988

© PRYOR PUBLICATIONS 1992
75 Dargate Road, Yorkletts, Whitstable,
Kent CT5 3EA, England.

Fax & Tel: 0227 274655

ISBN 0946014 12 4

Printed and bound by
Whitstable Litho Printers Ltd., Whitstable

CONTENTS

PREFACE.

IN entering upon this work I am fully conscious of the difficulty of battling against a long-existing and deep-rooted public prejudice. I only ask of my readers a fair hearing, an impartial consideration of my arguments, and an unbiassed judgment. If these be granted, I feel sure that many will be persuaded to make practical proof of the expe-

diency

diency of using insects as food. There are insects and insects. *My* insects are all vegetable feeders, clean, palatable, wholesome, and decidedly more particular in their feeding than ourselves. While I am confident that they will never condescend to eat *us*, I am equally confident that, on finding out how good they are, we shall some day right gladly cook and eat *them*.

INTRODUCTION

'EATING people' — so wrote Flanders and Swann in their popular musical *At the Drop of a Hat* — 'is wrong', a view few of us would dispute. Indeed, considering our omnivorous ape-like ancestry, the taboo against eating our own species is, fortunately, remarkably strong. But much more remarkable is the rejection by so many of us of most of the vast range of potentially edible things on earth.

We do not approach food rationally as fuel, and few of us really think about the nutritional value of what we eat and drink. Instead, our feeding habits are part of our culture. From black pudding to pickled jelly-fish, beauty lies in the eye of the beholder.

5   What

What we see and taste as beautiful depends largely on what our family and friends approve of — with just a little room for personal preference.

The concept of what is not acceptable as food in English culture is well conveyed by the school-boy's question 'What is worse than finding a maggot in your apple?' — 'Finding half a maggot.' Yet the maggot is clean, healthy, good protein and definitely edible. But from our earliest years we have been told that eating flies and ants is wrong. By the age of three most children have been firmly imprinted for life against insects, spiders, snails, slugs and worms by repetitive shouts of 'Dirty' from fond adults whenever an experiment is made with non-traditional food. Small wonder that at the age of six I disgraced myself at an aunt's table when offered a plate of winkles — and even as a young professional entomologist I could manage little more than a polite smile when

first

first offered Fortnum & Mason's Baby Bees in Syrup, or Chocolate-covered Grasshoppers.

Why Not Eat Insects? is not just a fascinating Victorian book, full of humour and ideas, it is also an interesting — indeed profound — question about human behaviour. In Europe we associate insect-eating arrogantly with lesser cultures. Australian aborigines are welcome to their Bogong Moth Balls — compressed handfuls of moths swept from their resting places beneath rocks and gently baked. People around the great lakes of eastern Africa can eat their Kungu Cake — myriads of midges pressed into a patty and cooked — we would prefer their fish as fodder.

But our culture is changing. Food in Britain has never been so diverse, and our feeding habits are increasingly adventurous. Perhaps the time is now ripe for insectivory to invade Chelsea; gently at first around Sloane Square, with Choux-fleurs garnis de Chenille,

7

Chenille, but in the further reaches of the King's Road surely the more discerning palates will find delight in the Curried Cockchafers or Grilled Grasshoppers and Wire-Worm Sauce recommended in this book?

LAURENCE MOUND

Keeper of Entomology
British Museum (Natural History)

May 1988

WHY NOT EAT INSECTS?

PART I.

WHY NOT?

"These ye may eat; the locust after his kind, and the bald locust after his kind, and the beetle after his kind, and the grasshopper after his kind."—LEV. xi. 22.

WHY not eat insects? Why not, indeed! What are the objections that can be brought forward to insects as food? In the word "insects" I here include other creatures such as some small mollusks and crustaceans which,

though

though not technically coming under the head of insects, still may be so called for the sake of brevity and convenience. "Ugh! I would not touch the loathsome things, much less eat one!" is the reply. But why on earth should these creatures be called loathsome, which, as a matter of fact, are not loathsome in any way, and, indeed, are in every way more fitted for human food than many of the so-called delicacies now highly prized? From chemical analysis it appears that the flesh of insects is composed of the same substances as are found in that of the higher animals. Again, if we look at the food they themselves live upon, which is one

of

of the commonest criterions as to whether an animal is, or is not, fit for human food, we find that the great majority of insects live entirely upon vegetable matter in one form or another; and, in fact, all those I shall hereafter propose to my readers as food are strict vegetarians. Carnivorous animals, such as the dog, cat, fox, etc., are held unworthy of the questionable dignity of being edible by civilized man. In the same manner I shall not ask my readers to consider for a moment the propriety or advisability of tasting such unclean-feeding insects as the common fly, the carrion beetle, or *Blaps mortisaga* (the churchyard beetle). But how

can

can any one who has ever gulped
down the luscious oyster alive at
three-and-sixpence per dozen, turn
up his nose and shudder at the
clean-feeding and less repulsive-
looking snail? The lobster, a
creature consumed in incredible
quantities at all the highest tables
in the land, is such a foul feeder
that, for its sure capture, the ex-
perienced fisherman will bait his
lobster-pot with putrid flesh or fish
which is too far gone even to
attract a crab. And yet, if at one
of those tables there appeared a
well-cooked dish of clean-feeding
slugs, the hardiest of the guests
would shrink from tasting it.
Again, the eel is universally eaten,

fried,

fried, stewed, or in pies, though it is the very scavenger of the water —there being no filth it will not swallow—like its equally relished fellow-scavenger the pig, the "unclean animal" of Scripture. There was once an equally strong objection to the pig, as there is at present against insects. What would the poor do without the bacon-pig now?

It is hard, very hard, to overcome the feelings that have been instilled into us from our youth upwards; but still I foresee the day when the slug will be as popular in England as its luscious namesake the Trepang, or sea-slug, is in China, and a dish of grasshoppers fried in butter as much relished by the

English

English peasant as a similarly treated dish of locusts is by an Arab or Hottentot. There are many reasons why this is to be hoped for. Firstly, philosophy bids us neglect no wholesome source of food. Secondly, what a pleasant change from the labourer's unvarying meal of bread, lard, and bacon, or bread and lard without bacon, or bread without lard or bacon, would be a good dish of fried cockchafers or grasshoppers. " How the poor live!" Badly, I know; but they neglect wholesome foods, from a foolish prejudice which it should be the task of their betters, by their example, to overcome. One of the constant questions of the day is,

How

How can the farmer most successfully battle with the insect devourers of his crops? I suggest that these insect devourers should be collected by the poor as food. Why not? I do not mean to pretend that the poor could live upon insects; but I do say that they might thus pleasantly and wholesomely vary their present diet while, at the same time, conferring a great benefit upon the agricultural world. Not only would their children then be rewarded by the farmers for hand-picking the destructive insects, but they would be doubly rewarded by partaking of toothsome and nourishing insect dishes at home.

After

After all, there is not such a very strong prejudice among the poorer classes against the swallowing of insects, as is shown by the survival in some districts of such old-fashioned medicines as wood-lice pills, and snails and slugs as a cure for consumption. I myself also knew a labourer, some years ago, in the west of England, who was regularly in the habit of picking up and eating any small white slugs which he happened to see, as tidbits, just as he would have picked wild strawberries.

It may require a strong effort of will to reason ourselves out of the stupid prejudices that have stood in our way for ages; but what is the

good

good of the advanced state of the times if we cannot thus cast aside these prejudices, just as we have caused to vanish before the ever-advancing tide of knowledge the worn-out theories of spontaneous generation and barnacle geese?

Cheese-mites, the grubs of a small fly, are freely eaten by many persons, whom I have often heard say "they are only cheese." There is certainly some ground for this assertion; as these grubs live entirely upon cheese; but what would one of these epicures say if I served up to him a cabbage boiled with its own grubs? Yet my argument that "they are only cabbage" would be fully as good as his.

As a matter of fact, I see every reason why cabbages should be thus served up, surrounded with a delicately flavoured fringe of the caterpillars which feed upon them. As things are now, the chance caterpillar which, having escaped the careful eye of the scullery-maid, is boiled among the close folds of the cabbage, quite spoils the dinner appetite of the person who happens to receive it with his helping of vegetable, and its loathsome (?) form is carefully hidden at the side of his plate or sent straight out of the room, so that its unwonted presence may no further nauseate the diners. Yet probably these same diners have, at the commence-

ment

ment of the meal, hailed with inward satisfaction the presence on the board of dozens of much more loathsome-looking oysters, and have actually swallowed perhaps a dozen of them raw and living as quite an appetizer for their dinner! At a table of gourmands, he who by chance thus gets the well-boiled larva served up in its own natural, clean food should, instead of being pitied for having his dinner spoilt, be, on the contrary, almost an object of envy, as he who gets the liver-wing. I am quite aware of the horror with which this opinion will be read by many at first sight, but when it is carefully thought over I fail to see that any one capable

of

of correct reasoning can deny its practical truth, even if he himself, though a frequent swallower of the raw oyster and a relisher of the scavenging lobster, continues to turn up his delicate nose at my suggestion to put it to a practical proof.

The general abhorrence of insects seems almost to have increased of late years, rather than diminished, owing, no doubt, to the fact of their being no longer familiar as medicines. At one time the fact of their being prescribed as remedies by village quacks and wise men made people, at any rate, familiar with the idea of swallowing them. Wood-lice, which conveniently roll

themselves

themselves up into the semblance of black pills, were taken as an aperient; centipedes were an invaluable specific for jaundice; cock-chafers for the plague; ladybirds for colic and measles. The advance of medical science and the suppression of wise folk have swept away this belief in the medicinal qualities of insects, except from out-of-the-way country corners, where a stray wise woman occasionally holds a divided sway with the parish doctor. As these theories die away, why should not the useful practice of using insects as food be introduced with advantage? From time to time letters appear in the papers inquiring as to the best method of

getting

getting rid of such insect pests as the wireworm, leather-jacket, chafer-grub, etc., and I have seen one method especially recommended. This is to set traps for the insect vermin by burying slices of turnip or potato stuck upon the ends of small sticks, whose other ends project from the ground to mark the spot. The slices, in the morning, will be covered with the mischievous ravagers, which, one answer went on to say, "may then be dealt with at pleasure." I say, then, collect them for the table. Man will often, in his universal selfishness, take the trouble to do acts, if they directly affect him or his stomach, which he would not

do

do for their mere utility; and if these wireworms, etc., were esteemed as articles of food, there would be a double incentive to the gathering of them. We have only to glance through the pages of Miss Eleanor Ormerod's excellent work on "Injurious Insects" to see what a power for harm lies in the myriads of the insect world, even if we do not know it from sad personal experience.

There cannot be said to be any really strong objection, among the upper classes, to making any new departure in the direction of foods, if it once becomes the fashion to do so. On page 25 is the *menu* of a dinner at the Chinese Restaurant at

the

the late Health Exhibition, whose quaint delicacies were eaten and well appreciated by crowds of fashionable people, who turn up their noses at the neglected supply of new delicacies at home.

Let us look into some of the items which these professedly most refined eaters partook of with relish —though it is only fair to state that some of the ladies could not sufficiently overcome their prejudices to enjoy their meal.

The "Bird's Nest Soup" was, I believe, universally appreciated, and, personally, I thought that it was perhaps the most delicious soup I had ever tasted. Yet, from what is it made, ye dainty feeders? The

nest

CHINESE RESTAURANT.

Menu, 11 Sept., 1884.

HORS D'ŒUVRE.
Pullulas à l'Huile.   Saucisson de Frankfort.
Olives.
Bird's Nest Soup.
Visigo à la Tortue.
Souchée de Turbot au Varech Violet.
Biche de Mer à la Matelote Chinoise.
Shaohsing Wine.
Petit Caisse à la Marquis Tsing.
Roulade de Pigeon farcie au Pistache.
Copeau de Veau à la Jardinière au Muscus.
Sharks' Fins à la Bagration.
Boule de Riz.
Shaohsing Wine.
Noisettes de Lotus à l'Olea Fragrance.
Pommes pralinée.   Compôte de Leechée.
Persdeaux Salade Romain.
Vermicelli Chinoise à la Milanaise.
Beignet Soufflé à la Vanille.
Gelée aux Fruits.
Biscuit Glace aux Amande pralinée.
Glace à la Crême de Café.
DESSERT.
Persimmons, Pommes Confit, Pêches,
Amands Vert, Grapes.
THÉ IMPÉRIAL.

nest of a small swallow, constructed by that bird principally by the means of threads of a viscid fluid secreted from its mouth. Does not that sound nasty enough? Yet what excellent soup is made therefrom, being not only delicious to the taste, but said also to possess great strengthening qualities, and to be an excellent specific for indigestion. The annual value of these nests imported into China and Japan exceeds £200,000. Surely, considering the general approbation expressed of this soup at the Health Exhibition, it would pay some enterprising London merchant to import nests into England.

The "Visigo a la Tortue" was

also

also an excellent soup, a kind of imitation turtle, made from the octopus or cuttle-fish.—The cuttle-fish! Go to any aquarium; look on those hideous creatures and tell me, are not they loathsome? Do they look nice to eat?

"Biche de Mer à la Matelote Chinoise."—This was the dish which frightened the more delicate ladies. Why? Merely because its common English name is the "sea slug." There cannot be a particle of doubt that, if it had always previously been known only by its less common name of sea cucumber or Trepang, it would have been refused by none. What's in a name? The Trepang by any

other

other name would taste as sweet! Those who partook of this dish all pronounced it to be excellent eating, although its ingredients did resemble in looks pieces of old shoe leather or large black slugs. Not that there could be any valid objection if it actually were made of either. Half the delicious calves' foot jelly in the world is made from old parchment and leather clippings, and slugs are no worse than oysters.

We have thus recently had an opportunity of tasting some of the varieties of a usual Chinese *menu*, and our verdict upon them was proved to be favourable by "the Chinese dinner at the Healtheries" becoming one of the fashionable

28   entertainments

entertainments of the season. There one had opportunities of watching, with wonder, the most refined ladies and gentlemen, in correct evening costume, sitting down to partake of a dinner, whose most attractive items, as shown in the *menu*, were such objects as bird's nest soup, cuttle-fish, sea slugs, and shark's fins, for no other reason than that it was the fashion to do so. I will venture to say that if it had been previously suggested to those people to have such items included in the *menu* at a country house, they would have expressed disgust at the idea. Fashion is the most powerful motive in the world. Why does not some one in a high

place

place set the common-sense fashion of adding insect dishes to our tables? The flock would not be long in following.

After eating of those unaccustomed dishes at the Health Exhibition, and discovering how good they were, is it not a wonder that people do not look around them for the many new gastronomic treasures lying neglected at their feet? Prejudice, prejudice, thy strength is enormous! People will dilate upon the delicate flavour of one fungus, under the name of mushroom, while they stamp upon, or cast from them, the disappointing young puff-ball and a dozen other common kinds of fungi, all equally nice and whole-

some,

some, if people would only recog-
nize it, as the one they gloat over.
People will, in like manner, enjoy
oysters and cockles, while they
abominate snails; they will make
themselves ill with indigestible and
foul-feeding lobsters while they
look with horror upon pretty clean-
feeding caterpillars. All this would
not be so absurd if it were only
the rich that were concerned, for
they can afford to be dainty. But
while we, in these days of agricultural depression, do all we can to
alleviate the sufferings of our starving labourers, ought we not to
exert our influence towards point-
ing out to them a neglected food
supply?

PART II.

INSECT-EATERS.

From almost every part of the inhabited globe instances and examples can be brought of the eating of insects, both in ancient and modern times, by people of every colour and nation. If I bring forward examples from ancient times, or from among those nations, in modern times, which are called uncivilized, I foresee that I shall be met with the argument, "Why should we imitate these uncivilized

races?"

races ?" But upon examination it
will be found that, though uncivilized, most of these peoples are
more particular as to the fitness
of their food than we are, and look
on us with far greater horror for
using, as food, the unclean pig or
the raw oyster, than we do upon
them for relishing a properly cooked
dish of clean-feeding locusts or
palm-grubs. If we are to imitate
in nothing these savage races, how
is it that from their example we
cultivate the priceless Peruvian
bark or quinine ; that we, rich and
poor alike, feed daily on the imported potato ; that we delight in
curry ; and that our men, each at
first struggling against his natural

D   33   aversion

aversion and sickness, accustom themselves by force of will to the soothing influence of the noxious weed, tobacco ?

Beginning with the earliest times, one can produce examples of insect-eating at every period down to our own age. Speaking to the people of Israel, at Lev. xi. 22, Moses directly encourages them to eat clean-feeding insects: " These ye may eat, the locust after his kind, and the bald locust after his kind, and the beetle after his kind, and the grasshopper after his kind." Again, John the Baptist is recorded to have lived in the desert upon locusts and wild honey. Some critics, however, apparently con-

sidering

sidering locusts unnatural food, and ignorant of how they are relished in the East, have gone out of their way to produce long arguments to prove that the word which has been translated "locusts" ought to have been rendered as the name of a species of cassia-pod. This is not so. Almost every traveller of note has given us an account of how the Eastern nations enjoy these insects. Pliny records the fact that in his day they were much eaten by the Parthians. Herodotus describes the mode adopted by the Nasamones of powdering locusts for the purpose of baking them into cakes.

The Hottentots, according to

Sparrman,

Sparrman, welcome the locusts as a godsend, although the whole country is devastated, for it is literally a case of the biter bit; and these locust-eaters grow round and fat from the incredible quantities they devour of their nutritious and appetizing persecutors. Cooked in many and various ways, locusts are eaten in the Crimea, Arabia, Persia, Madagascar, Africa, and India. Sometimes they are merely fried, their legs and wings plucked off, and the bodies eaten, flavoured with pepper and salt. At others they are powdered and baked into cakes ; or, again, they are boiled, turning red, like lobsters, in the process. In India, like every other

36   article

article of food, they are curried.*
In Arabia, Persia, and parts of
Africa there are regular locust
shops where they are exposed for
sale; and among the Moors they
are highly valued, appearing in the
menu at the best tables.   Their
method of cooking is to pluck off
the head, wings, and legs, boil for
half an hour, flavour with pepper
and salt, and fry in butter.   As I
can myself bear witness, of which
more hereafter, this recipe applied
to our English grasshoppers renders that despised insect a truly

* It has been cleverly suggested by Sim-
monds, in his "Curiosities of Food," that
their very name, *Gryllus*, is in itself an invita-
tion to cook them.

tasty

tasty morsel. From the time of Homer, the *Cicadæ* formed the theme of every Greek poet, in regard to both tunefulness and delicate flavour. Aristotle tells us that the most polished of the Greeks enjoyed them, considering the pupæ, or chrysalids, the greatest tid-bits, and after them the females heavy with their burden of eggs. Why this taste should have died out in modern Greece one cannot tell, for it is much more wholesome than many which have been assiduously perpetuated. *Cicadæ* are eaten at the present day by the American Indians and by the natives of Australia.

According to Pliny, the Roman

epicures

epicures were in the habit of fattening for the table the larvæ of the Cossus, with flour and wine. It is somewhat doubtful as to the exact identity of the insect represented by the word *Cossus;* but it was probably the large grub of the Stag Beetle (*Lucanus cervus*) or a large Longicorn Beetle (*Prionus corioranus*). The epicure of Rome was most dainty and discriminating in his food. Why, then, should we turn up our noses at what he considered as a great delicacy?

Ælian tells us that in his time an Indian king served up, for his Greek guests, as dessert, a dish of roasted grubs, extracted from some tree or plant, which were considered

by

by the natives a great treat.
There is very little doubt that these
were the larvæ of the palm weevil
(*Calandra palmarum*), huge grubs
as large as a man's thumb, which
are, at the present day, extracted
from the palm trees and eaten with
great relish by the negroes in the
West Indies under the name of
Grugru. Kirby in his "Entomology" says that a certain Sir
John La Forey, who was somewhat
an epicure, was extremely partial to
this grub when properly cooked.

The family of Longicorn Beetles
affords a rich store of luscious
larvæ, which are sought and eaten
by the inhabitants of most countries
where they are to be found in any
40   abundance.

abundance. As I mentioned before, it is considered by some to
have been a member of this family
(*Prionus corioranus*) that was fed
up by the Romans for the table
with all the care that is nowadays
bestowed upon a prize pig. One
of this tribe is also mentioned by
Madame Merian as being eaten by
both the native and white inhabitants of Surinam, who serve
them up nicely roasted after being
emptied and washed. In St. Pierre's
voyages also, this, or some similar
insect, is mentioned, under the
name of the Moutac grub, as being
eaten by whites and natives alike.
In Java there is a species of Cockchafer (*Melolontha hypoleuca*) to

which

which Wiedemann has drawn attention, as forming food for the inhabitants. The last instance from among the *Coleoptera* I will bring forward is the well-known meal worm, the larvæ of a small beetle (*Tenebrio*), which Turkish women eat in large quantities for the purpose of acquiring that plumpness of form their lords so much admire. The Chinese, making use of "the worm, a thing that crept on the bare earth, then wrought a tomb and slept" as food, eat the chrysalids of the silkworms after the silk has been wound from off the cocoons. They fry them in butter or lard, add yolk of eggs, and season with pepper, salt, and vinegar. A certain

Mr.

Mr. Favand, a Chinese missionary, says that he found this food refreshing and strengthening. Dr. Darwin, also, in his " Phytologia," mentions this dish, and says that a white earth grub and the larvæ of the sphinx moths are also eaten, which latter he tried, and found to be delicious. The Hottentots eat caterpillars, both cooked and raw, collecting and carrying them in large calabashes to their homes, where they fry them in iron pots over a gentle fire, stirring them about the while. They eat them, cooked thus, in handfuls, without any flavouring or sauce. A traveller who on several occasions tried this dish, tells us that he thought it

delicate

delicate, nourishing, and wholesome, resembling in taste sugared cream or sweet almond paste.

Passing now from the strictly insect world, I come to some common land mollusks, which have formed, and indeed form at the present time, food for many nations as cultivated as ourselves, but which we, strong in insular prejudice, still refuse. Pliny tells us how snails were appreciated in Ancient Rome, and were cultivated and fed to increase their number and size for the table. It is almost too well known to need mention, that in most parts of Europe at the present time snails are extensively eaten and enjoyed. No precedent ought,

44   surely,

surely, to be needed for the adoption
of snails as food, when we copy
and justly appreciate in almost
every other particular the cookery
of France. Still, if English stub-
born natures wish for a precedent
from their own beloved island they
can have it, for Lister, in his
"Historia Animalium Anglicæ," says
that in his time snails were served
up at table, boiled in spring-water,
and seasoned with oil, pepper, and
salt.

Even Spiders have been relished
as tid-bits, not only by uncivilized
nations, but by Europeans of culti-
vation. For Reaumur tells of a
young lady who was so fond of
spiders that she never saw one

without

without catching and eating it. Lalande, the French astronomer, had similar tastes; and Rosel speaks of a German who was in the habit of spreading spiders, like butter, upon his bread. This taste I do not in any way uphold, for the preying spider, which devours his fellow-insects, whether foul feeders or no, should be avoided, as are carnivorous beasts in our animal diet.

I think that I have now produced a sufficient number of precedents for the eating of insects, both in ancient and modern times, by nations civilized and uncivilized. These ought to be sufficient to incite any person of ordinary

46   strength

strength of mind to try for himself
the unknown delicacies around him.
We pride ourselves upon our imitation of the Greeks and Romans
in their arts ; we treasure their dead
languages : why not, then, take a
useful hint from their tables ? We
imitate the savage nations in their
use of numberless drugs, spices, and
condiments : why not go a step
further ?

Part III.

PART III.

WE have seen that, from the time of Moses down to the present day, various members of the insect family of *Orthoptera*, which includes the locusts, crickets, and grasshoppers, have been and are eaten and appreciated in many parts of the world. Now let us look at home, and consider why we should not do likewise, adding to our tables that clean meat, " the

48   grasshopper

grasshopper after his kind." We
are not without precedent. The
example of the Church has backed
up the written permission of the
Bible. The Rev. R. Sheppard,
many years ago, had some of our
common large grasshoppers served
up at his table, according to the
recipe used by the inhabitants of
Morocco in the cooking of their
favourite locusts. Here it is.
" Having plucked off their heads,
legs, and wings, sprinkle them with
pepper and salt and chopped
parsley, fry in butter, and add some
vinegar." He found them excellent.
From personal experiment I can
fully endorse his opinion ; and there
are few who would not, if they

E 49 would

would but try this dish. I have eaten them raw, and I have eaten them cooked. Raw, they are pleasant to the taste; cooked, they are delicious. The above recipe is simple; but any one with a knowledge of cookery would know how to improve upon it, producing from this source such dishes, say, as "Grasshoppers au gratin," or "Acridæ sautés à la Maître d'Hôtel."

Among the *Coleoptera*, or Beetles, we find many which might well serve as food; some in their larval, some in their complete state, and some in both. Here, again, there is no need to recruit from among the ranks of the carnivorous or foul

feeders

feeders. There are, without those, plenty of strict vegetarians.

The grub of the Stag Beetle (*Lucanus cervus*) is said by many, as before mentioned, to be identical with the Cossus, which the Romans used to fatten for the table upon flour and wine. As this destructive grub, before turning to its beetle stage of life, spends some years gnawing at the hearts of our oak trees, it would be a boon to timber growers if this taste of the Romans were revived. There are many varieties of these timber-borers which might well be used for food, as are the Grugru and the Moutac grub in the East and West Indies. I have especially noticed a plump white

white grub which infests our young sallow trees in great numbers, boring upwards from the foot of the stem. When the plantations are cut down, why should this delicacy be wasted? If foolishly rejected at the tables of the rich, these larvæ should be a joy to the woodman's family, and a reward for the toil of the breadwinner. If this were so, it would be the means of keeping down the number of these destructive pests, which are not now considered worth collecting.

What valid objection can there be to eating these insects, when the larvæ of similar beetles are eaten all over the world, both by natives

and

and by whites, and when such larvæ are unanimously pronounced to be wholesome and palatable?

The Meal-worm, the larva of a small beetle (*Tenebrio*), is generally looked upon with disgust, as only fit food for tame birds. Even the strong-stomached and hungry sailor will rap his sea-biscuit on the table to shake out the worms before eating it. Let him shake out the worms, by all means; but let him collect them, fry in lard, and spread the dainty upon his dry biscuit. He will not again throw Meal-worms away.

In the common Cockchafer (*Melolontha vulgaris*) we find an inveterate enemy, which, after spending

three

three years in gnawing the roots of our clover and grasses as a huge white grub, turns to its beetle state, only to continue its ravages upon the foliage of our fruit or forest trees. Literally tooth and nail we ought to battle with this enemy, for in both its stages it is a most dainty morsel for the table. The birds are more sensible than we. They know well the value of the fat chafer as food. With what joy the jaunty rooks, following the plough with long strides over the upturned clover lea, pounce upon the luscious grubs! What a feast the birds have among the swarms of chafers in the tall tree-tops!

Erasmus Darwin, in his " Phyto-

logia,"

logia," says : " I have observed the house sparrow destroy the May-chafer, eating out the central part of it, and am told that turkeys and rooks do the same ; which I thence conclude might be grateful food, if properly cooked, as the locusts or termites of the East. And probably the large grub, or larva of it, which the rooks pick up in following the plough, is as delicious as the grub called Grugru, and a large caterpillar which feeds on the palm, both of which are roasted and eaten in the West Indies." Here is the openly expressed opinion of one of our greatest philosophers and deepest thinkers ; and there is not the slightest doubt that it is correct.

55   Again

Again I endorse from personal experience. Try them, as I have; they *are* delicious. Cockchafers are not only common, but of a most serviceable size and plumpness, while their grubs are, when full grown, at least two inches in length, and fat in proportion.

What a godsend to housekeepers to discover a new *entrée* to vary the monotony of the present round! Why should invention, which makes such gigantic strides in other directions, stand still in cookery? Here then, mistresses, who thirst to place new and dainty dishes before your guests, what better could you have than "Curried Maychafers"—or, if you want a more mysterious title, " Larvæ Melolonthæ à la Grugru " ? Land-owning guests ought to welcome the opportunity of retaliating, at your table, under the " lex talionis," upon this, one of the worst of their insect tormentors. Another dish, which should take with the farmer, would be " Fried Chafers with Wireworm sauce." Perhaps, how-ever, the little word " worm " might be objected to. So let us pander to the refined senses of the delicately fastidious by writing it upon our *menu* as " Fried Melolonthæ with Elater sauce." I know that wire-worms are an excellent substitute for shrimps. There are, also, thou-sands of members of the same

family

family as the shrimp (*Crustaceans*) in every garden, namely, the common Wood-lice (*Oniscus muriarius*). I have eaten these, and found that, when chewed, a flavour is developed remarkably akin to that so much appreciated in their sea cousins. Wood-louse sauce is equal, if not distinctly superior to, shrimp.

The following is the recipe: Collect a quantity of the finest woodlice to be found (no difficult task, as they swarm under the bark of every rotten tree), and drop them into boiling water, which will kill them instantly, but not turn them red, as might be expected. At the same time put into a saucepan a quarter of a pound of fresh butter, a teaspoonful of flour, a small glass of water, a little milk, some pepper and salt, and place it on the stove. As soon as the sauce is thick, take it off and put in the wood-lice. This is an excellent sauce for fish. Try it.

Passing on to the order *Hymenoptera*, the Sawfly at once strikes us as a very familiar insect, which in its larval stage plays sad havoc among the gooseberry bushes, often stripping them bare of leaves, and thus spoiling all chance of fruit. We all know in what myriads the grub swarms upon the trees, and how hard it is to induce our gardener, or any one else, to take timely steps for its destruction. If it were

59   known

known to be nice to eat, there would
be little fear of this voracious feeder
carrying on its destruction uninter-
rupted.   It would be a race between
the cook and the gardener's wife,
who should first arrive at the poor
gooseberry bush.   There is also
the Turnip Sawfly, better known
to farmers as "the Black," which
sometimes devours whole fields of
roots, leaving not a leaf to be seen.
In this order are included Bees
and Wasps. From the former we
already derive a delicious sweet in
the form of golden honey. From
the latter we might, if we chose,
derive an equally delicious savoury.
What disciple of old Izaak Walton,
when he has been all the morning

enticing

enticing the wily trout with luscious wasp grubs baked to a turn, has not suspected a new and appetizing taste imparted to his midday meal of bread and cheese or sandwich? Perhaps his own meal has travelled to the scene of action in the same basket as the rich cakes of grubs; or it may be that the fish are biting too well to allow time for a thorough hand-washing, and rapid bites are taken from the lunch in the intervals between the bobbing of the float and the replacing of the nibbled grubs. At any rate, it will, sometimes, so happen to every fisherman to get the taste and smell of cooked wasp grubs with his meal, and I have never noticed that it in any way

spoilt

spoilt his appetite. Attracted by the said taste and smell, and having no prejudices against insect food, I have myself spread the baked grubs upon my bread, and found their excellent flavour quite sufficient to account for the fondness of the trout for this particular bait. I will admit that wasps are occasionally carnivorous, but it is the exception and not the rule. Moreover, the saccharine fluid with which they feed their infant grubs is, I believe, entirely composed of vegetable juices, drawn from ripe fruits and flowers. Their babes, like our own, are fed only upon what are called "spoon victuals." Let us, then, welcome among our new

insect

insect dishes "Wasp grubs baked in the comb." The number of wasps' nests taken and destroyed, in a prolific season, is something extraordinary. I have known as many as sixteen or twenty nests to be taken by a gardener within a very short radius round his house. What a waste of good wholesome food takes place then, when cake after cake, loaded with fat grubs, is stamped under foot! The next order, the *Lepidoptera* (butterflies and moths), is rich in material for practical experiment and demonstration of my theory of insect food for omnivorous man. The usual stock terms for insects, "hideous," "loathsome," etc., can-

not

not be applied with any justice to this class, which, in its perfect state is renowned for its elegant beauty, and in its larval or caterpillar state is almost invariably pleasingly coloured and by no means repulsive to the eye. Their diet, too, is of the most purely vegetarian description, consisting, as it does, in the first stage of leaves, and the sweet nectar of flowers in the second. The tiny ant knows and appreciates the sweetness of insects which feed upon the juices of plants or flowers, for it keeps and tends with care numerous milch herds of aphides or green flies, to coax from their plump bodies the pearly drops of the honey dew it loves so well.

We

We have always been taught that in many points the ant is to be imitated. In its just appreciation of insects as a sweet source of food it is to be imitated too. I think it is in "Swiss Family Robinson" that there is a clever account of some travellers, wandering at night through a forest by torchlight, being greatly annoyed by huge moths, which repeatedly extinguished the torches by their suicidal love of light. However, annoyance was turned to joy when, tempted by the appetizing smell of the toasted moths, the hungry travellers ventured to satisfy in part their hunger with the suicides, which they found as excellent in flavour as in smell.

From what I recollect of the tale, I believe this was quite a fancy description, probably founded on the real habits of the natives which had been observed by the travelled author of the book. I well remember that, on reading that account, my youthful imagination reproduced without effort the appetizing smell of a plump baked moth ; but it did not occur to me then to try such a tid-bit. Lately, however, I have done so, to find the dream of my childhood fully realized as to the delights, both in taste and smell, of a fat moth nicely baked. Try them, ye epicures ! What possible argument can be advanced against eating a creature beautiful without and

66   sweet

sweet within ; a creature nourished on nectar, the fabled food of the gods ?

In attempting to reconcile the popular taste to the consumption of this same order in its larval stage as "caterpillars," a more difficult task perhaps awaits me. But why ? I never could thoroughly understand the intense disgust with which the appearance at the dinner-table of a well-boiled caterpillar, accidentally served with cabbage, is always greeted. The feeling is purely one of habit, and the outcome of unjust prejudice. These delicate, shuddering people, who now, with appetites gone, push away their plates upon the appear-

67   ance

ance of a well-cooked vegetable-fed caterpillar, have probably just swallowed a dozen live oysters; or they may have partaken of the foul-feeding lobster, and are perhaps pleasantly anticipating the arrival of a dish of ungutted woodcock! I have pointed out before that we have Dr. Darwin's authority that the caterpillars of the sphinx moths, as eaten by the Chinese, are very palatable; and another traveller has told us that he found the caterpillars eaten by the Hottentots tasted like almond paste. Of course, in choosing caterpillars for eating, it is necessary to discriminate between those feeding on poisonous and non-poisonous plants;

but

but there is no more difficulty in this than in distinguishing between the edible and poisonous in berries or fungi.

The caterpillar pests swarming in our kitchen gardens, which might with advantage be collected for food, are really too numerous to be fully described here, but I will point out a few of the best; at the same time calling attention to the fact that they all feed upon the wholesome vegetables which we cultivate for our own eating. To begin, the large white cabbage butterfly (*Pontia brassicæ*) is one of our most familiar butterflies. Its caterpillar, when full-grown, is one and a half inches in length, and,

owing

owing to its unpleasant habit of living upon his cabbages, of which it usually leaves nothing but skeleton leaves, is too well known to every gardener. It is of a greenish colour upon the back, yellow underneath, striped with yellow along the back and sides, spotted all over with black, and covered more or less with tiny hairs. Miss Eleanor Ormerod * says, with reference to these pests, " Hand-picking the caterpillars is a tedious remedy, but where there is no great extent of ground, it is advisable as a certain cure."

This effectual remedy would no longer be looked upon as tedious

* " Manual of Injurious Insects."

if

if the fruits of the picking were to form a dish for the gardener's dinner, or appear in the *menu* of his mistress as "Larvæ Pontiæ à l'Hottentot." Again she says, "When the first brood of caterpillars are full-grown, and have disappeared from the cabbages in early summer, they have left them to turn to chrysalids in any sheltered nook near, and may be collected in large numbers by children for a trifle per hundred. They may be chiefly found in outhouses, potting-sheds, and the like places, in every neglected corner, under rough stairs, step-ladders, or beams or shelves, or fastened against rough stone walls or mortar." Why

should

should we not imitate the Chinese, who, as I have stated, eat the chrysalids of silkworms ?

Silkworms feed on the mulberry, lettuce, etc. ; these caterpillars upon the homely cabbage. Let us, then, cast aside our foolish prejudice, and delight in chrysalids fried in butter, with yolk of eggs and seasoning, or " Chrysalids à la Chinoise."

The foregoing remarks apply equally to the small white cabbage butterfly (*Pontia rapæ*), whose caterpillars are smaller, of a green colour, and velvety, having a stripe of yellow along the back, and spots of the same colour along the sides.

Sticking still to cabbage, we next have the cabbage moth (*Mamestra brassicæ*),

72

brassicæ), whose caterpillar is perhaps more generally known as a forward intruder at table than any other. The larva is about an inch and a half in length, varies a great deal in colour, from dirty flesh to green, and is smooth and naked-looking. Its constant habit of gnawing right down into the heart of any cabbage or cauliflower attacked renders it a great nuisance in the garden, and also accounts for its frequent, and at present uninvited, appearance in a boiled state at the dinner-table.

It was the accident of his house and pigstye being burnt to the ground that first introduced the flavour of the luscious, but unclean,

73   pig

pig to the celestial Chinamen. Let these minor accidental appearances at table make us acquainted with the flavour of the clean and wholesome caterpillar, and let not the silent appeal be in vain of these martyrs, who invite us to profit by their martyrdom. Let us not, with a shudder, hide the evidence of their sacrifice under a temporary shroud of vegetable, but rather let us welcome these pioneers of future delicacies with smiles and open arms.

Continuing the list, I will next mention the large yellow underwing moth, whose caterpillar feeds upon turnip and cabbage leaves. The moth itself is a very familiar sight,

74   its

its size and yellow underwings rendering it a conspicuous object when, disturbed from its day retreat, it rises with sluggish flight before us. In seasons when this moth is numerous great numbers might be caught, both in the daytime and at night, with the net and by sugaring trees as practised by moth-collectors. When nicely fried in butter, their plump bodies rival the torch-cooked delicacies of the traveller's tale. Again, there is the common Buff-tip, a handsome moth, with forewings of a beautiful grey colour, marked with ruddy and black patches, and tipped, as its name imports, with light buff. It is handsome. What is more, let me whisper the ogreish suggestion that

that its body, an inch in length, is plump, round, and sweet. Its caterpillars are well known to every one, whether Londoner or countryman, for they swarm, at the end of June, in town and country alike upon their favourite lime trees. Their yellow forms, striped and ringed with black, are often to be seen crawling across the arid desert of the London pavements in search of some congenial soil wherein they bury themselves for the term of insect purgatory. Looking up then at the tree from which these wanderers have descended, one may see branches, perhaps many, perhaps few, stripped of their foliage and down the stem other caterpillars hurriedly crawling,

76   knowing

knowing that their time has come; that nature calls them to throw off their gay garments and humble themselves beneath the soil, before bursting out into rollicking Buff-tips. It never strikes the Londoner, as he hurries along beneath the shady trees, that these caterpillars are good to eat. He either stamps upon or carefully avoids them, according to his nature. The street boy picks up, plays with, and finally squashes them; but the extraordinary part of it is that it never strikes him to taste them. Boys taste almost everything. But this prejudice against insects seems rooted in them from the earliest age, for I have never seen a child experiment

upon

upon the unknown sweets of insect food. These Buff-tip caterpillars swarm upon the trees in such numbers, in favourable seasons, that many a dish can be obtained with a little trouble, which is amply repaid not only by their flavour, but also by the saving of the tender foliage of the limes. Most of the commoner moths which flit in thousands by night, around our fields and gardens, have nice fat carcases, and ought certainly to be used as food. Why, they are the very incarnescence of sweetness, beauty, and deliciousness ; living storehouses of nectar gathered from the most fragrant flowers ! They, too, voluntarily and suggestively

78   sacrifice

sacrifice themselves upon the altar of our lamps, as we sit, with open windows, in the balmy summer nights. They fry and grill themselves before our eyes, saying, "Does not the sweet scent of our cooked bodies tempt you? Fry us with butter; we are delicious. Boil us, grill us, stew us; we are good all ways!"

I will now pass on to our British land mollusks, beginning with the snail, of which it has been said, "As the fisherman hates the otter, so does the gardener this voracious, destructive pest." Anathematized by every person who possesses the smallest patch of garden; lying in abundance around our feet, a wholesome food, and

79   at

at the same time a pest to be destroyed, they are still almost entirely neglected by rich and poor alike, though the rich long for new dishes to tempt their jaded palates, and the poor starve. This is the more extraordinary when it is considered how fond the whole nation is of such mollusks as it is in the habit of eating. To the rich there are no greater delicacies than oysters, while the poor consume incredible quantities of the cheaper mollusks, such as cockles, whelks, etc. One has only to walk down the streets of any poor quarter of London to realize the immense trade which is done by the numerous costermongers, whose barrows are

laden

laden with little plates of ready-cooked mollusks, of many varieties. Yet in the country the poorer labourers and their families go on week after week, attempting to keep body and soul together with nothing but bread, varied, if possible, by the addition of a taste of bacon, while hundreds of nutritious and wholesome snails and slugs swarm at night upon the little cottage garden. Why this wanton and reckless waste of food? Prejudice, foolish prejudice! Half the poor of England would actually die of starvation before stretching out their hands to gather the plentiful molluscous food which their neighbours in France delight in. There are many

cases—I have known several myself
—where the poor will gather snails
and small slugs, and swallow them
raw, as a remedy for cough or weak
chest; yet it never seems to strike
them that this strengthening medicine is quite plentiful enough to
serve as a pleasant and strengthening food.   As a medicine, they are
right to eat their mollusks raw,
because snails and slugs, like all
their class, consist principally of
albumen which when raw is easily
digested.

Of course the rich can afford to
please themselves and reject a
pleasant, wholesome food if they
choose; but it seems a sin that our
starving poor should continue to

neglect

neglect this abundant food-supply.
Something could be done by force
of example. Masters might prepare
savoury snail dishes, according to
the recipes used in all parts of the
Continent, and in course of time the
servants would follow suit. One
great stumbling-block in the way is
the generally prevailing idea that
there is only one species, the edible
snail (*Helix pomatia*), which is fit
for food, or used as such upon the
Continent. It cannot be too widely
known that this is quite a mistake.
The only superiority of the so-
called edible snail over its fellows
is its superior size. The fact of its
superiority in size recommended it
to the Romans as the best species

to

to cultivate for the table; the fact of it having been so favoured and cultivated above its fellows has given rise to its name, and to the false idea that none other is edible. This *Helix pomatia* is by no means common in England, but is found in Kent, Surrey, and other southern counties, where it is supposed by many to have been imported by the invading Romans.

The common garden snail (*Helix aspersa*), as well as many other smaller kinds, is eaten in France and everywhere else where snails find favour.

The real fact is that all our species of snails are edible, unless they are gathered fresh from feeding upon

84   some

some poisonous plant. To avoid this danger, it is usual either to starve the snails or to feed them upon wholesome herbs for some days previous to preparing them for the table. The Romans, we read, used to fatten their snails upon meal and new wine until they attained an enormous size and excellent flavour. At the present day in Italy, they are sometimes kept in bran for some time before being eaten. In many places upon the Continent there may be seen snail-preserves, or *escargotières*, consisting of odd corners of gardens enclosed with boards and netted over the top. In these enclosures hundreds of snails are kept and fed

upon

upon wholesome vegetables and such herbs as impart to their consumers an agreeable flavour. I should like to see a simply constructed snail-preserve in every cottage garden in England. Further information on the subject will be found in an excellent work, " Edible British Mollusks," by G. M. S. Lovell, from which I take the following recipes, the excellency of which I can personally vouch for.

1. *To dress snails.*—Snails that feed on vines are considered the best. Put some water into a saucepan, and when it begins to boil throw in the snails and let them boil a quarter of an hour ; then take them out of their shells, wash them

several

several times, taking great pains to cleanse them thoroughly, place them in clean water, and boil them again for a quarter of an hour. Then take them out, rinse them and dry them, and place them with a little butter in a frying-pan, and fry them gently for a few minutes sufficient to brown them; then serve with some piquante sauce.

2. *Snails cooked in the French way.*—Crack the shells and throw them into boiling water, with a little salt and herbs, sufficient to make the whole savoury. In a quarter of an hour take them out, pick the snails from the shells, and boil them again; then put them into a sauce-pan, with butter, parsley, pepper,

87   thyme,

thyme, a bay-leaf and a little flour. When sufficiently done, add the yolk of an egg well beaten, and the juice of a lemon or some vinegar.

Now, don't you think those recipes sound nice ? I have eaten snails raw, and I have eaten them cooked. Raw, they are nourishing, but almost flavourless ; nicely cooked, they are excellent. It is of no use for me to attempt to describe their delicate taste. Try them for yourselves, and judge.

We do not find many instances of slugs being generally eaten, unless as a remedy for lung diseases ; but I fail to see why, seeing how nearly they are allied to snails, they should be so generally neglected. I have

known

known two gardeners who were in the constant habit of picking up and swallowing any small grey slugs they happened to see. One gave as his reason for so doing, that he thought his chest was weak ; the other, that he liked them : both honest enough reasons. The poor might make most nutritious soup and palatable dishes from the common varieties of slug, which, left to themselves, do so much damage to farm and garden crops.

The great grey slug (*Limax maximus*), the red slug (*Limax rufus*), the black slug (*Limax ater*), and the small grey slug are all to be found in great numbers in most parts of England, and when

89   properly

properly cooked are all equally good. People who walk the fields and gardens in the daytime wonder at the immense havoc played by slugs, of which they see so comparatively few. Let them, however, go out at nightfall, with a good bull's-eye lantern, and they will see, advancing upon their crops from rubbish heaps, from hollow trees, from crevices in walls, and from every conceivable hiding-place, hosts of slugs, grey, black, red, large and small. Why should not these be gathered in hundreds and thousands by the poor for food? The larger varieties might be treated like the Chinese delicacies, the sea-slugs, cut open and

dried

dried for keeping. Slugs may be secured without the trouble of a night attack, by placing garden refuse or cabbage leaves under the shelter of boards or tiles. To these traps the slugs will come in the night to feed, and, finding themselves sheltered when day breaks, will remain there to be caught, instead of returning to their usual strongholds.

Let not the labourer say, "We starve. Meat is too dear; bread is almost as dear because the wire-worm, the leather-jacket, and the May-bug worm have thinned the crop; our little stock of flour is rendered useless by meal-worms. The caterpillars swarm upon our

cabbages

cabbages; the sawfly has spoilt all chance of the gooseberries we hoped to sell: hosts of great slugs and snails have devoured what the others left. Upon our fruit trees the cockchafers are gnawing the leaves to bareness."

Yes, meat is dear; but the wheat crop would have been twice as thick if the wireworms, the leather-jackets, and the luscious white chafer grubs had been diligently collected by you for food. Meal-worms are fattening. You should have hand-picked your cabbages and gooseberry trees, so that you might enjoy and profit by their would-be destroyers. The snails and slugs ought to be welcome, and

sought

sought for, to be placed in your little snail-preserve. As for cockchafers, you ought to get sixpence a score for them from the squire's housekeeper. They are, like mushrooms, to be gathered and sold as delicacies; or you could fry them for your own suppers, before they have a chance of baring your poor fruit trees. Thus you would not only save all the produce of the little garden, but also pleasantly vary your monotonous meal with wholesome and savoury dishes.

Nature, if undisturbed, balances all her creatures against each other so that no one individual kind shall, increase and multiply to an undue extent. This principle has been

summed

summed up in the quaint lines—

> " Big fleas have little fleas
> Upon their backs to bite 'em ;
> Little fleas have smaller fleas,
> And so on, *ad infinitum*."

When not interfered with, Nature's whole machinery works with perfect regularity, and her balance is exactly poised. If, however, we presume to intermeddle, the whole system soon becomes deranged. By importing or cultivating fancy fruits unnatural to the soil, we have interfered with the machinery ; by killing the birds to protect these fancy fruits, we destroy Nature's balance of her creatures—for birds are the natural counterpoise to insects. In consequence we have,

to

to the great detriment of our crops,
an overweight and undue increase
of insects. To save them from
their devourers, we must throw
some extra weight into the opposite
scale to compensate for the loss of
the birds we kill. I have done my
best to show how this weight may
be added, and how the balance may
be restored.

On the following pages I have
sketched out two *menus*, comprising
some specimen dishes which may be
made from insects. Of course these
menus are unnaturally crowded with
insect items; but they are merely
intended to show how such dishes
may be usefully introduced into the
chief courses of an ordinary dinner.

I.

I.

FRENCH.

Menu.

Potage aux Limaces à la Chinoise.

Morue bouillie à l'Anglaise, Sauce
aux Limaçons.

Larves de Guêpes frites au Rayon.

Phalènes à l'Hottentot.

Bœuf aux Chenilles.

Petites Carottes, Sauce blanche aux
Rougets.

Crême de Groseilles aux Nemates.

Larves de Hanneton Grillées.

Cerfs Volants à la Gru Gru.

I.

I.

ENGLISH.

Menu.

Slug Soup.
Boiled Cod with Snail Sauce.

Wasp Grubs fried in the Comb.
Moths sautés in Butter.
Braized Beef with Caterpillars.
New Carrots with Wireworm Sauce.

Gooseberry Cream with Sawflies.
Devilled Chafer Grubs.
Stag Beetle Larvæ on Toast.

II.

II.

FRENCH.

Menu.

Potage aux Limaçons à la Française.

Soles frites, Sauce aux Cloportes.

Hannetons à la Sauterelle des Indes.

Fricassée de Poulets aux Chrysa-
lides.

Carré de Mouton, Sauce aux Rougets.

Canetons aux Petits Pois.

Choufleurs garnies de Chenilles.

Phalènes au Parmesan.

II.

II.

ENGLISH.

Menu.

Snail Soup.

Fried soles, with Woodlouse Sauce.

Curried Cockchafers.

Fricassée of Chicken with Chrysalids.

Boiled Neck of Mutton with Wire-
worm Sauce.

Ducklings, with Green Peas.

Cauliflowers garnished with Caterpillars.

Moths on Toast.

Don't:

A Manual of Mistakes & Improprieties
More or Less Prevalent in Conduct & Speech

Don't, a best seller of the early 1880s, is a reflection of a society long since past and makes interesting and amusing reading now.

This is a copy of the original, measuring 4½" x 5½" and contains such diverse advice as:

DON'T say "hung" when "hanged" is meant. Men, unfortunately, are sometimes hanged; pictures are hung.

DON'T say "lady" when you mean wife.

DON'T be servile towards superiors.

DON'T wear diamonds in the morning.

Sixth reprint.

Over 42,000 copies sold.

Price £3.⁵⁰
inc. postage

English
As She is Spoke:

or

A Jest in Sober Earnest.

. . . is a rich selection from one of the funniest books in the English language—in fact one of the funniest books *about* the English language.

The book derives from *Pedro Carolino's "Guide to the Conversation in Portuguese and English,"* published in 1869. It seems Carolino's knowledge of English was little more than that furnished by a French–English dictionary. It was a greater contribution to humour than linguistics.

Apart from the cover, this book is a facsimile of "Andrew Tuer's" extracts from Carolino's work published in 1883, which went to ten editions.

Price **£3.00**
inc. postage